KENTUCKY
WIDE

JEFF ROGERS PANORAMICS

RatDog Publishing
Lexington, Kentucky

Photography by Jeff Rogers
Design and production: Sumo Design
Introduction: Patti Edmon
Photo editing: Jeff Hancock
Marketing research: Sally Evans
Art consultant: Joe Petro III
Transparency scans: Richard Sisk
Transparency film processing: The Film Lab
Printing: Moonlight Press
Never-ending support and patience: Sally Rogers

Library of Congress Control Number: 2005910285

ISBN 0977240002, hardbound 1st edition
ISBN 0977240003, limited edition of 100, handbound with one original print. For more information,
contact the photographer.

Printed in China For Moonlight Press

Jeff Rogers Photography, Inc. 859.255.9917 www.JeffRogers.com
P.O. Box 368 Lexington, Kentucky 40588-0368

KENTUCKY
WIDE

JEFF ROGERS PANORAMICS

Dedicated to the Dream Giver

This book was created without any commercial
endorsements, supplies or support.
Deo est Gloria!

A NOTE FROM THE PHOTOGRAPHER

I love getting lost. This book is the result of time spent wandering the towns and back roads of Kentucky. Growing up in Corinth, Kentucky, a town with a population of 250, gave me an appreciation for rural communities, the way of life and the land. My fondest memories are of fishing, shooting and just being outdoors. The afternoons I wasn't scheduled to work at the filling station, I'd hop in my beloved 1966 Chevy II (Nova) SS and drive around the countryside with my "groundhog gun." I didn't often stop to take a shot, though I did acquire a passion for the intense beauty of the landscape.

Art has always been a part of my life. My mother is an accomplished artist and she nurtured my creativity at an early age. I was introduced to photography while working toward my art degree at Transylvania University; I was immediately hooked, and promptly traded my .44 Ruger Super Blackhawk handgun for my first camera, a manual 35mm SLR.

Light is essential to the quality of a photograph, but I believe a successful image depends upon composition, most likely a result of my art background. I actually tried to improve my early prints by trimming them with scissors! I spent countless hours in the darkroom, often cropping to achieve the desired effect, but still work to frame the desired elements with a minimum of distraction.

Black and white photography was my first favorite, and along the way I've experimented with infrared, images with a Diana toy camera, gicleé canvases from digitally painted color images.

I have used and owned a variety of cameras ranging from 35mm, to medium and large format, even an 11x14 view camera. Each has its own personality and portal to the images they help create. I acquired my first panoramic camera about ten years ago. *See more under Technical Notes .*

I photographed a number of these images while on commercial assignment but most were the result of being lost. My favorite time to shoot is in the quiet peace of the early morning hours; there is a different ambience before the sun rises and the fog is burned off. Quite a few of these images are meditations taken during intimate, predawn moments with the Creator. I hope this book brings you peace and gives you a greater appreciation for the beauty in the world we affectionately call the Bluegrass.

KENTUCKY WIDE:
A PANORAMIC NARRATIVE OF KENTUCKY

by Patti Edmon

A photograph is a fleeting moment, captured with a click of the shutter. The artist's vision is rendered in that fraction of a second and the composition changes as the horse spooks and gallops from the fence, the sun shifts altering light and shadow. The resulting image then, is a frame in the narrative of the photographer's life.

The panoramic photograph can also be considered a narrative. The wide arc of the lens affords a multitude of possibilities not available in the conventional format. Taking full advantage of a camera that sees such a broader span of information, and often at different angles, requires the cultivation of a new way of seeing, a panoramic viewpoint.

Natural instinct is to center the subject in the frame, with the intention, even, of cropping peripheral 'distractions.' The panoramic format, however, presents an entire scene as subject. Jeff Rogers embraced the need to consider the collection of elements across the broader spectrum, how they enhance and interact. This careful study of composition has resulted in images that are as cohesive as they are complex in detail.

In addition to posing a unique creative challenge, a panoramic image is closer in width to the capacity of human vision. Removing the barriers imposed by medium, and even large format lenses, is akin to taking off "the blinders" and we are drawn into the photograph with a rewarding intensity.

An entire landscape can be encompassed in a single glance, but appreciating the details is only possible with an extended reading. Indeed, sweeping 'stories' have been conveyed in a single canvas in cultures throughout history. For millennia the Chinese painted scrolls in a similar, exaggerated rectangular format, to be studied left to right. Prehistoric life was rendered in drawings across the expanse of a cave wall, and medieval battle scenes depicted on tapestries.

The first panoramic images were made not long after the invention of photography, in 1839, by pasting together two or more Daguerreotype plates. Named for the inventor, Louis-Jacques-Mandé Daguerre, the process was cumbersome and highly sensitive but made available the first means for capturing a "truthful likeness." Early panoramas depicted historic events and geography, vistas of wilderness and cities remarkable in width and detail.

Imagine Union generals and military experts poring over the 10.5 x 42 inch wide images shot by George Barnard atop Lookout Mountain in Tennessee, in 1864. The ability to examine the terrain and fortifications of a Confederate territory must have seemed nothing short of magic.

Panoramic photography reached the height of popularity at the turn of the twentieth century, thanks to the development of faster, less expensive photographic processes and the large, stationary-lens 'banquet' camera, so named for its presence at enormous dinner parties, conventions and other gatherings.

More than four hundred photographers' panoramic works have been preserved and cataloged by the Library of Congress. It is possible to view the crowds gathered in the stands at Churchill Downs in 1921 and again in this book, seventy-five years later, for the 1996 running of the Kentucky Derby. Jeff chose the unique vantage point of the famed twin spires, truly a bird's eye view that intensifies the atmosphere of the event. While panoramas are still used to render landscapes and large crowds, Jeff is among the recent artists who have pushed the medium far beyond historic boundaries.

A hundred people might walk the same path and no two will see it in precisely the same manner. Perhaps that's the true value of this collection; as an artist, Jeff Rogers has been refining, deepening his way of seeing the world around him for more than twenty years. Each photograph represents a fresh and original narrative from his panoramic point of view; the essential, rare beauty of Kentucky is conveyed in spiritual, compelling vistas that the untrained eye might miss.

Kentucky is a faithful subject, as rich in diversity as it is in beauty. The preservation of historic, cultural and natural resources are the foundation for a thriving tourism industry that has been an economic stronghold since the state's earliest days. What better example than the horse, for which Kentucky is known across the globe. Whether circling the paddock at Churchill Downs, grazing in a rural pasture at dawn or in the snow-covered foreground of a multimillion-dollar breeding farm, Jeff has captured the rare qualities that have lured artists and Hollywood film crews for decades. An examination of these images reveals a sense of place that is both timeless and constantly evolving.

For a moment we, too, can travel back in time, to pause for a horse drawn carriage in the village at Shakertown. Admire the sunrise at Cumberland Gap, the light painting a vast expanse of trees in vibrant fall colors. Or look out over the Red River Gorge, as Daniel Boone, arguably the state's first tourist, might have, awestruck at the wave of rising fog not yet burned off by the morning sun.

Through his viewfinder, Jeff explores and interprets Kentucky's narrative, told over the years by the rock fences built in the early to mid nineteenth century, a rural store that was once the heart of a tiny community, the tobacco season, from planting, blooming, to cutting and hanging sticks to dry in barns across the state.

Jeff's belief in the "landscape greater than the eye can see," offers a visible connection between the water that gradually, gracefully carves at the rock in the Big South Fork of the Cumberland River, and the force behind its creation. The images in Kentucky Wide are the result of Jeff's unique skill and panoramic vision; innumerable hours spent communing with the Creator, walking familiar paths and forging a few of his own.

PLATE 1

PLATE 2

PLATE 4

PLATE 5

PLATE 6

PLATE 7

PLATE 9

PLATE 10

PLATE 11

PLATE 13

PLATE 14

PLATE 15

PLATE 16

PLATE 17

PLATE 18

PLATE 20

PLATE 21

PLATE 22

PLATE 23

PLATE 24

PLATE 25

PLATE 26

PLATE 27

PLATE 29

PLATE 30

PLATE 31

PLATE 32

PLATE 33

PLATE 34

PLATE 35

PLATE 37

PLATE 38

PLATE 39

PLATE 40

PLATE 41

PLATE 42

PLATE 43

PLATE 44

PLATE 47

PLATE 48

PLATE 49

PLATE 50

PLATE 51

PLATE 53

PLATE 54

PLATE 55

PLATE 57

PLATE 58

PLATE 59

PLATE 60

PLATE 61

PLATE 62

PLATE 63

PLATE 65

PLATE 66

PLATE 68

PLATE 69

"¿Podrías hacerme un jersey?", le preguntó la ballena. Sería MUCHO trabajo, pero Bootsy quiso intentarlo.

Cuando Bootsy llegó a donde
tenía el cesto, no encontró la lana.

Pingüino se dio cuenta de que él también tenía el costurero vacío.

Los dos pingüinos se pusieron a buscar.

"¿Has visto mi lana?", preguntó Bootsy.
"No", dijo Pingüino. "¡Yo tampoco
encuentro la mía!"

Mientras tanto, iban haciendo calceta para estar abrigados.

Incluso la hacían para los amigos mientras recorrían el camino.

Hacían calceta para divertirse.

Hacían calceta
para sentirse confortables.

Y esto puso muy contentos a Pingüino y Bootsy, hasta que . . .

. . . se levantó una ventolera
que separó a los dos pingüinos.

Ahora el camino era largo, y solitario . . .

Bootsy siguió el rastro bajo la lluvia,

bajo la nieve,

y soñaba que llegarían días mejores.

"Espero volver a verte",
pensó Pingüino mientras dejaba
una señal para Bootsy.

Hicieron calceta de un pico a otro
mientras la lana iba alargándose cada vez
más. Subían cada vez más.

Hasta que al final . . .

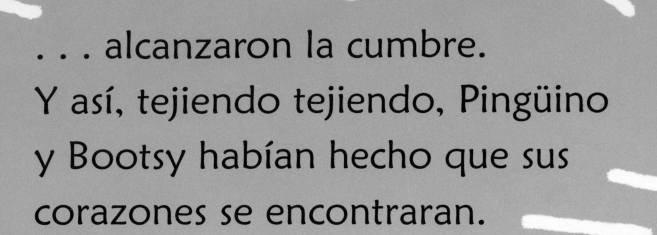

. . . alcanzaron la cumbre.
Y así, tejiendo tejiendo, Pingüino
y Bootsy habían hecho que sus
corazones se encontraran.

PLATE 70

PLATE 71

PLATE 72

PLATE 73

PLATE 74

PLATE 75

LIST OF PLATES

TECHNICAL NOTES

As an artist, it is imperative to stretch and grow. I have had the opportunity to work with a variety of different camera formats and systems. Trying to "see" and experience life through the viewfinder of a panoramic camera is not only rewarding, but very challenging. The images in this book are not photographs that have been simply cropped, but were created with three particular types of panoramic cameras. My first panoramic camera was a V-Pan 617, which is a specially modified view camera (utilizing view camera movements and lenses) that has a large film magazine that accommodated either 120 or 220 roll film. Next, I began using a Noblex 120, a rotating lens camera that has a field of view almost as wide as that of our human eyes. Last, I have used a Hasselblad XPan camera, which is a 35mm camera that can switch back and forth from panoramic to normal perspective mid-roll. Even though I am known as a pioneer in the world of digital photography, all of the images in this book were shot with traditional transparency film.